Made in United States
North Haven, CT
03 May 2023

36174798R00057